Rendering unto Caesar

Examining What Jesus Said About Giving God What Is His

Chris Surber

Energion Publications
Gonzalez, FL
2014

ISBN10: 1-63199-067-5
ISBN13: 978-1-63199-067-0

Energion Publications
P. O. Box 841
Gonzalez, FL 32560

energion.com
pubs@energion.com
850-525-3916

CHAPTER 1

WHAT JESUS SAID - EXPOSITION

RENDERING TO CAESAR

Then the Pharisees met together to plot how to trap Jesus into saying something for which He could be arrested. They sent some of their disciples, along with the supporters of Herod, to meet with Him. "Teacher," they said, "we know how honest You are. You teach the way of God truthfully. You are impartial and don't play favorites. Now tell us what You think about this: Is it right to pay taxes to Caesar or not?" But Jesus knew their evil motives. "You hypocrites!" He said. "Why are you trying to trap Me? Here, show Me the coin used for the tax." When they handed Him a Roman coin, He asked, "Whose picture and title are stamped on it?" "Caesar's," they replied. "Well, then," He said, "give to Caesar what belongs to Caesar, and give to God what belongs to God." His reply amazed them, and they went away. (Matthew 22:15-22)

This is the theological basis for all that follows and really the central matter at hand. What does it mean to render to Caesar what is his and render to God what is His? How a believer understands this text will to a large degree determine how they will approach matters of nationalism and politics as they follow Jesus. It is at the very least a strong indicator for how one understands the basic tenets of the personal relationship mandated in the New Testament between living a Christian life and living as a citizen in a particular nation. What does it mean to render unto Caesar?

This passage is usually seen as essentially about paying taxes. While that is what is on the surface of the discussion between Jesus

1

and the Pharisees, the core principles contained in the words of Jesus point us toward the deeper matter of how to render to Caesar what is rightfully his without denying God what is rightfully His. This passage is not really about paying taxes at all. Seldom is any of Jesus' teaching not infused with richer meaning than what is on the surface and easily gleaned from a superficial reading of the text. When we consider the historical context, the situation, and crowd to whom Jesus was speaking, it becomes clear that there is more to what Jesus is saying.

In the historic context of Jesus day He could have easily been identified as an enemy of Rome if He has simply answered the Pharisees' question: "No it is not lawful to pay taxes to Caesar." On the other hand He would have alienated the Jewish people to whom He was preaching and teaching if He had responded: "Yes you should pay taxes to the foreign occupiers that everyone distrusts and hates." It was the perfect question on the part of the Pharisees and they knew it. They must have had an inclination as to Jesus' answer to think they could trap Him this way. It is assumed in their question that they already had a good idea that Jesus' radical, Kingdom of God message would be at war with the idea of strong allegiance to kingdoms of this world. They must have already had an idea of how Jesus might respond.

Wrapped up in Jesus' response is much more than a simple affirmation of paying taxes. Jesus highlights His own poverty in the fact that He has to ask for someone to give Him a coin bearing the Emperor's image – a denarius. Follow Jesus and you may not even have money with which to pay taxes. His Kingdom is not of or about this world. Jesus points out that the image upon the coin is that of the Emperor. It is quite literally "his coin." It was the coin appropriate for paying the government tax in that day. The Pharisees don't care about the moral imperatives of their question. They just want to snare Jesus in a political trap. So Jesus shifts the conversation into other worldly eternal matters. He asks "Whose image is on the coin?"

Of course the Pharisees would have been aware that God prohibits false images in the first commandments of Moses. Jesus is highlighting the truth that God has already commanded a total heart's allegiance from His people to Himself. This passage of Scripture points to matters far deeper than the practical matter of the legality or morality of paying taxes. Jesus' response points us to the very nature of a true and proper relationship with the world for the child of God. In other words, Jesus doesn't really affirm paying taxes nor does He condemn it. He uses the opportunity to point His people in the direction of disentanglement with worldly affairs.

In a deeply insightful article on this subject, Jeff Barr puts it this way.

> Jesus tells His interrogators, "Render therefore to Caesar the things that are Caesar's; and to God, the things that are God's." This response begs the question of what is licitly God's and what is licitly Caesar's. In the Hebrew tradition, everything rightfully belonged to God. By using the words, "image and inscription," Jesus has already reminded His interrogators that God was owed exclusive allegiance and total love and worship.[1]

Jesus is clearly not saying that it is central to the Christian life to go out of his or her way to render a portion of their life or belongings or allegiance to Caesar. In this instance Caesar is representative of the world. Jesus' statement is in fact a response to a question intended to trap Him into saying something overtly political, which would have been inherently contrary to the way of Jesus. He commented time and again on the sin of people and the need for the nation of Israel as a people to repent, but he never did so in a way that connected spiritual repentance, national spiritual

---

1   "Lewrockwell.com," Jeff Barr, accessed December 10, 2013 March 17, 2010, http://www.lewrockwell.com/2010/03/jeffrey-f-barr/ render-unto-caesar-amostmisunderstood-newtestamentpassage.

identity, or any other spiritual matter with the global, national, or local politics of His day.

The Pharisees' only concern here, as it is noted in every instance where this encounter occurs in the gospels (Mark 12, Luke 20), is to give cause for continued harassment of Jesus. The religious Jews apparently would gladly see that harassment come from them or the state. They didn't care where it came from so long as Jesus was silenced. They wanted to trap Jesus. They would have, as they ultimately did, use the hammer of the state to crush Jesus whom they envied and feared. Even here we see that religion without Jesus has an inherent inclination toward garnering the state as its moral ambassador. The scheming and plotting of the Pharisees also highlights their inability to separate the spiritual kingdom that Jesus proclaimed and their obsession with socio-political power and religious control.

The way of Jesus is counterintuitive to the way that religious people always look at the best ways to influence the world. Religion – outside of the pure way of Jesus – always places a high premium on control. It's far easier to subjugate society through moral oppression than it is to serve society the way Jesus did. The entire point of this passage is to point disciples of Jesus toward total and abject surrender to God of everything that belongs to Him. So what belongs to Him?

My old self has been crucified with Christ. It is no longer I who live, but Christ lives in me. So I live in this earthly body by trusting in the Son of God, who loved me and gave Himself for me. (Galatians 2:20)

You have died with Christ, and He has set you free from the spiritual powers of this world. So why do you keep on following the rules of the world? (Colossians 2:20)

4

This is a trustworthy saying: If we die with Him, we will also live with Him. (2 Timothy 2:11)

What belongs to God? Everything that encompasses our life, our death, our affections, our desires, our goals, our longings, and our allegiances we are to render to God. If we are in Christ they are His. When we withhold them we are not keeping what is ours. We are robbing things that belong to God. Our life is hidden with God in Christ and consequently our willful actions are supposed to reflect His intentions through us in the world. Not only is Jesus not saying that a portion of our allegiance belongs to the world and a portion belongs to God, He is saying let Caesar keep his idols of self-worship for himself while you surrender all that you are to God.

This is the central tenet of Jesus teaching and it's the very thing the Pharisees either couldn't or simply refused to grasp. It's the very thing that many of us don't get today. It kept them from salvation in Christ. It keeps us from spiritual victory in Christ. It kept them in their religion. It traps us in half-Christianity; claiming allegiance with Christ in our hearts while everything about our lives says that we are rendering our lives to Caesar. Here's what I mean.

The average Christian Evangelical today is so concerned with subjective experience that he has forgotten, or never learned anything of, what I will call his trans-generative nature. That is, the average Christian reads passages like those I've cited above through a purely personally subjective experiential lens. Consequently, the deepest essence of Kingdom meaning is lost on him. We read that our old self has been crucified with Christ and it is Him that lives in us, and we immediately think of our own ability to conquer sin subjectively. Christ lives in me so I should be able to abstain from eating that last donut (gluttony) or looking at that girl crossing the street in such a provocative dress (lust).

There certainly is a present aspect to Christ living in us. However, the deepest meaning has more to do with the coming and present Kingdom than it does with present sin. Our ability to conquer sin is a byproduct of the metaphysical reality that has taken place in the life of the born again believer. It isn't merely that we have identified with Christ in His death and been metaphorically reborn to new life. We have died and the life we live in the body we live in Christ. We have been bought with a price and the lives we live no longer belong to us.

Our identity in Christ means that we are no longer a part of this world.

When we get a sense of this reality, deeply inwardly practical questions of how to relate to the world become less difficult to answer. Our acute sense or awareness of how we do and don't fit into the world's patterns and paradigms becomes intuitive. We are strangers and pilgrims in this world. We are no longer part of this world. The radical difference between Kingdom citizens and world citizens couldn't be more striking. But this is more than just doing a few different things. Wrapping our minds around this is about reshaping our entire perspective, attitudes, and identities. This is bigger than a few choices made for Jesus. This is about how we understand who we are – in Him.

One of the hardest things I ever had to do in my life was to leave the Marine Corps. I didn't realize it at the time but when I left active service, I left behind an identity. I didn't wear a Marine Corps uniform for nearly a decade without becoming a Marine in the deepest parts of my self-understanding. It was who I was. It was how I understood myself. Being a Marine defined my place in the world. Not only that, but my identity was rewarded and reinforced. I liked the respect I received from perfect strangers when in uniform. I liked the sense of belonging to something bigger than myself with a respected history and tradition all its own.

As hard as it was to leave that identity behind, it is harder yet to leave behind our identity in this world when we are stripped out of it by the grace of God. Many believers never do lose their old identity. Granted, it's a constant struggle and we'll never be perfectly apart from this world until we are entirely out of it by death or the return of Christ. But there is a temptation that many succumb to, I think. They say what I've just said as an excuse to war against the catastrophic shift in our perspective that salvation brings. We hang on to our heart's affections for the things we belong to in this world, though we have been taken out of this world and placed into Christ.

What we are addressing here is identity. Who is Jesus? Who am I? Who am I in light of who Jesus is? A central theme of what I'm offering in this treatment of this subject is simply this: **guard your heart**. God is at work shaping believers into the perfect image of Christ. "And I am certain that God, who began the good work within you, will continue His work until it is finally finished on the day when Christ Jesus returns" (Philippians 1:6). The last thing we need to do is to succumb to political pandering and have our image shaped by the culture of the world. Don't give Caesar what isn't his – your heart.

THE GREAT COMMISSION

Jesus came and told His disciples, "I have been given all authority in heaven and on earth. Therefore, go and make disciples of all the nations, baptizing them in the name of the Father and the Son and the Holy Spirit. Teach these new disciples to obey all the commands I have given you. And be sure of this: I am with you always, even to the end of the age. (Matthew 28:18-20)

A GLOBAL BORDERLESS MANDATE: ALL NATIONS

The heartbeat of the Church is the glory of God. God saves us in order to glorify Himself through us. The Church, it may be well stated, is the instrument through which God's glory is shone into the world. The primary means of spreading the glory of God in the world is the Great Commission. The mission of the church is simple. Be disciples. Make disciples. Global evangelism starts in our communities and local regions and then it extends to the uttermost parts of the earth. Gathering the nations into the embrace of God through saving faith is the primary task and function of every local church in the world.

For many people in America, Caesar has taken what isn't his. Our affections and identity as followers of Jesus are wrapped up in our identity as Americans. We are keepers of local religious tradition rather than participants in God's plan of redemption for the entire world. We've not guarded our hearts from falling too much in love with the systems around us. As a result, our categories are fused together. Instead of God being revealed in the Church in this country, God and country go together like eggs and bacon in the idolatrous, gluttonous minds of the American Church.

The most obvious conflict with the fusion of Christian and American identity is that it denies the universal nature of the Kingdom of God. When our allegiances are too strongly aligned with any kingdom of this world, be it the relatively benevolent kingdom of America or a malevolent kingdom like Nazi Germany, it takes away from our ability to reflect the unique beauty of Christ in the world through our lives. Discipleship is costly. It costs us the identity that we had before Christ broke into our lives and snatched our affections away from this world for Him.

In order to glorify God, we need a Gospel that preaches everywhere. Our Gospel needs to preach in Beverly Hills and the hills of Haiti. Our Gospel needs to preach to Liberal and Conservative. Our Gospel is for the lost, of which we are all a part. In the hearts of many American Christians there is a subtle and sometimes overt bitterness for the rest of the world. We are Americans. We want to keep our money local. We want to keep the American economy strong. We have fused our identity as Americans with our identity as Christians and consequently we miss the reality of our global Kingdom citizenship.

While it is not the case everywhere of course, I have personally seen many members of local churches balk as the notion that an inherent part of the local church's responsibility includes spreading the Gospel to foreign lands. In the work that my family and I do in Haiti, we have garnered the support of many like-minded,

8

missions-minded friends. We have also felt the venomous sting of harsh criticism of our motives and of the wrongheaded assumptions about why Haitians are in the plight that they are in as a people. It's not just Haiti, of course. I've heard and read these kinds of comments about many parts of the world.

Here are a few of the more common and memorable comments:

"Haven't they ever heard of birth control? Why doesn't some mission agency help them stop having kids so they can feed the ones they have?"

"They've already heard the Gospel. Don't they worship Satan in voodoo?"

"Is it wise to take your children there?" (In a tone that said, "It surely isn't!")

"Why send our money overseas when there are so many problems and needs here in America?"

"If they weren't so lazy, they wouldn't need our help."

"Let the missionaries preach the Gospel to them. I've got family *here* who haven't even come to a saving knowledge of God in Christ."

The only thing more dangerous than a lie is a half-truth. We too often focus on the part that is true and rationalize the lie its wrapped in. People around the world are people. Do they not have the same right that Americans consider "unalienable" to pursue life, liberty, and happiness? Nowhere does God call His Church to castrate poor people in order to limit the number of poor people. Very much to the contrary Jesus said, "You are the salt of the earth. But what good is salt if it has lost its flavor? Can you make it salty again? It will be thrown out and trampled underfoot as worthless" (Matthew 5:13).

The poor among us are a part of the inherent plan and sovereign allowance of God. Their lives, just like your life and mine, have inherent value and God-honoring purpose. "You will always have the poor among you, but you will not always have Me" (Matthew 26:11). Our mission and mandate is not to limit their numbers but to win them to Christ for salvation. In heaven the masses celebrate the worth of God.

Our mission, as I've mentioned above, is to gather the nations into the embrace of God so that we increase the abundance of those bringing glory to God in this world. We do that by any means necessary. In Burkina Faso, Africa, one of the poorest parts of West Africa, I have friends who are sponsoring kids in schools in order to witness to the power of God's love. As a result, the missionaries who go there have a wide open door to spread the Gospel among the people. I have another friend who translated the Bible into Salvadoran sign language and lived among the people. By investing her life into the lives of Salvadorans, she was able to shine the light of Jesus Christ into their world. In Haiti, we use feeding clinics, among other tools, to create communities of friends so that we can bring the Gospel to them for salvation and follow-on discipleship.

When we are called from darkness to light, we are also called out of primary allegiance with the place of our national origin. We become citizens of Heaven. We don't cease to be members of a nation but we become something that supersedes all national boundaries. We become children of God. In 2009, I made my first pilgrimage to Israel. It was fantastic. While I had studied church history in seminary and personal study, walking the streets of Jerusalem opened my eyes to the history of the Bible like I could not have experienced any other way. Walking on those ancient streets and along the shore of the Sea of Galilee, gave me a lasting sense of connection to the biblical narrative. The crazy thing is I've been homesick for Israel ever since.

I'm not from Israel but my story is. My story and your story started in a garden and culminated in an empty tomb. My story and your story took place in Israel where the God of the Universe broke into the world in the man Yeshua, Jesus of Nazareth. That place is a shadow of my home. Israel is the place where the promises of Heaven and an eternal kingdom were given. Our home is not this world and it surely isn't the place of our national birth. For every believer, we have a global borderless mandate to gather the children of God into the embrace of God.

There are needs in America and we should strive to meet them. There are needs in Africa, Russia, Haiti, Peru, and all over the globe and our heart should break everywhere there is poverty and injustice. But most of all, you and I should seek the specific leading of God to the part of the world where He has set aside a group of people on a hill, who are waiting for us to come and shine the light of Christ into their lives. To do that, we've got to see ourselves as Kingdom citizens. God's calling on your life may be in Kentucky but it may be in Athens. The question is not why I should send my money overseas. The question is: Where is God calling me – as a citizen of His kingdom – to shine the light of Christ and will I obey Him and trust His sovereign wisdom or lean on my own?

A GLOBAL SPIRITUAL MANDATE: MAKE DISCIPLES.

The mandate and mission of every follower of Jesus is inherently spiritual. The task of every Christian and local church is to win the lost to Christ. We do this through using our spiritual gifts, our time, our talents, our financial treasure, and every opportunity presented to us to shine the light of Christ and share His truth. Our mission is not of this world. We are pilgrims, strangers, and sojourners in this life. We are not defenders of the traditional American way. Neither are we heralds of a new modern more liberal way of life that has come to set men free from the tyranny of a bygone era.

We are a third thing, other than Conservative or Liberal, Republican or Democrat. We are torch bearers in a dark world that needs Christ for salvation. The aim of our spiritual weapons of love and truth are the hearts of men for the glory of God.

Jesus said "I am with you always." He said He must ascend to the Father so that the Paraklete, the Helper, the Holy Spirit may come. Our mission is essentially spiritual. I mentioned above that in places like Haiti we meet the physical needs of people so that

11

we can earn trust, display the love of God, and open a door for the Gospel. The Church is God's instrument to lead sinners to Him, not essentially to reform society. We are citizens of a soon coming Kingdom, not reform agents.

The difference between (social) morality and (Christian) righteousness cannot be overstated. The Church cannot make a righteous society, though we may influence its morality. Today, society just bucks against what it perceives to be our judgment on people who think differently, even when the difference is the difference between what God says is right and what society says is acceptable. We are fighting the wrong wars with the wrong enemies when we war against the society instead of Satan. Our global mandate is to live spiritually empowered lives and bear fruit for the Kingdom.

Guard your heart. Don't mistake bringing goodness to society for bringing glory to God. God isn't glorified in our muddled efforts to make a more Christian society out of a society of largely non-Christians. This is how we glorify God. "My Father is glorified by this, that you bear much fruit, and so prove to be my disciples" (John 15:8). Bearing fruit is the way we glorify God because "It is of the very essence and outflow of [Christ's] life."[2]

When we engage the world on its terms, we lower ourselves to its battles. Our mission is to win individuals and people groups to salvation in Christ and make of them disciples who can replicate what has happened in their lives by the power of the Holy Spirit. "The place where the Christian stops to refuel is prayer."[3] It is not in the latest debate over the most recent hotly contested social battle. The world's battles are life-taking. When our fuel for life is the power of the Holy Spirit and our battle is for souls in love with the truth of Christ as our weapon, we find meaning and purpose in our doing.

---

2   James E. Rosscup, *Abiding in Christ* (Grand Rapids: Zondervan, 1973), 64.

3   Leonard Ravenhill, *Revival Praying* (Minneapolis, Minnesota: Bethany Fellowship, 1962), 55.

When we set aside the spiritual mandate of our mission for the worldly porridge of politics and nationalism, Caesar will keep taking what isn't his – our energy and our affections.

BEING SALT AND LIGHT

You are the salt of the earth. But what good is salt if it has lost its flavor? Can you make it salty again? It will be thrown out and trampled underfoot as worthless. You are the light of the world – like a city on a hilltop that cannot be hidden. No one lights a lamp and then puts it under a basket. Instead, a lamp is placed on a stand, where it gives light to everyone in the house. In the same way, let your good deeds shine out for all to see, so that everyone will praise your heavenly Father. (Matthew 5:13-16)

There is a difference between being salt and light and being salt in wounds. The world is full of hurting people. Are we leading them to the Light for healing or pouring salt in their sin? The mission of the Church has nothing to do with any national agenda or political parties' goals. By definition there can never be a political party in this world that is purely a party for the interests of Christians because Jesus came to inaugurate a completely different kind of Kingdom.

The famous sermon given by Jon Winthrop, on the precipice of the Pilgrims' landing in the New World and founding the Massachusetts Bay Colony, has left an indelible mark on the identity of America, especially American Christianity. In the sermon entitled "A Model of Christian Charity," Winthrop cited Jesus' words from Matthew 5:14 and drew a parallel to their endeavors in creating their own City on a Hill by way of their colony that would be a seminal undertaking ultimately leading to our nation. His sermon paved the way for American exceptionalism and the notion that we are the New Israel in the world – the idea that we are God's country.

How tragic for future generations of Christians! While America has been used of God in so many wonderful ways, Christians growing up in America have been befuddled by the myth that to be an American is to be Christian. We have received a cultural heritage that makes the distinctly spiritual nature of Jesus' words in Matthew 5:14 difficult to comprehend and apply. Our biblical interpretation has been tainted by our national heritage; even though that heritage has many wonderful aspects to it.

What does it mean to be salt and light? Much has been written and said to address this question. My point here is simply to point the reader toward the inherently spiritual and other worldly aspects of these commands. The context is in the Sermon on the Mount and immediately follows the Beatitudes. In the very section of the Scripture following the salt and light (City on a Hill) passage, Jesus describes His purpose for coming into the world! He says this: "But I warn you—unless your righteousness is better than the righteousness of the teachers of religious law and the Pharisees, you will never enter the Kingdom of Heaven" (Matthew 5:20)!

This passage of Scripture was not given by Jesus so that generations later the Puritans could lay the groundwork for the myth of the Christian exceptionalism of America. Jesus used this analogy of a city on a hill to make the point that as citizens of His kingdom we are not to hide the light of Christ from anyone or place it under anything – including dimming our witness of it by fusing it with nationalism and national political ideologies of any type. We are salt in the world. Our calling is to preserve truth in a world full of systems of domination based upon and filled with lies. Light cannot be soiled, just as the truth of Christ, and our witness to it, must be kept pure.

Salt preserves and light expels the darkness. That's our mandate in the world. God isn't calling us to make a better version of society but to be a society of Jesus' followers, who shine the light of truth. When our allegiances are too closely aligned to the kingdoms of this world our witness to the Kingdom of God is dimmed and our preserving impact as salt loses its affect. "So Jesus calls his disciples to exert a double influence on the secular community, a negative influence by arresting its decay and a positive influence by bringing light into its darkness."[4] Guard your heart. Keep your national identity separate from your Kingdom identity in order to keep it pure.

> *Jesus answered, "My Kingdom is not an earthly kingdom. If it were, My followers would fight to keep Me from being handed over to the Jewish leaders. But My Kingdom is not of this world."*
>
> (John 18:36)

> *Jesus spoke to the people once more and said, "I am the light of the world. If you follow Me, you won't have to walk in darkness, because you will have the light that leads to life."*   (John 8:12)

When our affections are tangled in the world's systems and we don't see ourselves as an "other" kind of preservative and cleansing influence, how can we shine light and sprinkle salt into the corrupt kingdom systems of the world? Light is by definition pure. It breaks into and expels the darkness. Salt must be kept separate in order to maintain its effectiveness.

---

4   John R. Stott, *The Message of the Sermon on the Mount* (Downers Grove, Illinois: Inter-varsity Press, 1978), 64.

CHAPTER 2

HOW TO HAVE PEACE
IN THE WORLD

EXPLANATION

Guard your heart. That is a recurrent theme in this discussion. "I have told you all this so that you may have peace in Me. Here on earth you will have many trials and sorrows. But take heart, because I have overcome the world" (John 16:33). My strongest interest is that you, the reader, would take away from this discussion a growing fervor for living in the soul-satisfying peace that God has provided for His children through the Holy Spirit for life in this world. This world is full of wars for us to fight. But to fight them surrounded by and indwelt by the peace of God, we've got to engage the actual enemy in ways that are consistent with the weapons of our warfare.

When we engage the wrong enemy with the right weapons, we will lose the battles. When we engage the right enemy with the wrong weapons, we will also lose. We need to align our spiritual weapons with the spiritual wars we were intended to fight. Too many Christians are wearing the right armor but fighting the wrong battles. As a result, the armor weighs them down and they live non-victorious lives filled with frustration instead of peace.

DON'T BE A CULTURE WAR CASUALTY

Battle axes don't belong on harvest fields. Sadly, many Christians today approach the spiritual battles that wage all around us in our land and in the world from a purely worldly vantage point.

As a result, we are losing the wars. In Romans 1:13-18 the Apostle Paul writes:

> *I want you to know, dear brothers and sisters, that I planned many times to visit you, but I was prevented until now. I want to work among you and see spiritual fruit, just as I have seen among other Gentiles. For I have a great sense of obligation to people in both the civilized world and the rest of the world, to the educated and uneducated alike. So I am eager to come to you in Rome, too, to preach the Good News. For I am not ashamed of this Good News about Christ. It is the power of God at work, saving everyone who believes – the Jew first and also the Gentile. This Good News tells us how God makes us right in His sight. This is accomplished from start to finish by faith. As the Scriptures say, "It is through faith that a righteous person has life." But God shows His anger from heaven against all sinful, wicked people who suppress the truth by their wickedness.*

I want you take note of three specific principles wrapped up in this passage of Scripture.

» Paul's primary interest is seeing spiritual fruit among believers.
» He is not ashamed of the Gospel and recognizes its power and purpose to save people of every nation for eternity from start to finish by faith.
» God is the one rightly angered because of sinful unbelief.

These three ideas, recurrent throughout the Bible form the foundation of how the Church is called to interact with itself and the world. Let's consider them.

There is something very wrong in the Church today when the focus of so many believers is to win the nation back for God in a Bill O'Reilly-like, angry-morality-tirade, rather than to embody the character traits that Jesus gave His disciples in the Sermon on the Mount.

17

"God blesses those who are poor and realize their need for Him, for the Kingdom of Heaven is theirs. God blesses those who mourn, for they will be comforted. God blesses those who are humble, for they will inherit the whole earth. God blesses those who hunger and thirst for justice, for they will be satisfied. God blesses those who are merciful, for they will be shown mercy. God blesses those whose hearts are pure, for they will see God. God blesses those who work for peace, for they will be called the children of God. God blesses those who are persecuted for doing right, for the Kingdom of Heaven is theirs. "God blesses you when people mock you and persecute you and lie about you and say all sorts of evil things against you because you are My followers. Be happy about it! Be very glad! For a great reward awaits you in heaven. And remember, the ancient prophets were persecuted in the same way."

(Matthew 5:3-12)

The Beatitudes are widely and historically recognized in the Church to be the benchmark gold standard for Christian conduct. These are the characteristics that should define our relationships within the Church and with the outside world. Jesus tells us to be the kind of people who sense our need for God above all else. Should we not look to God for protection and provision, rather than making a primary objective of the Church the garnering of political authority through the installment of "our" candidates into the offices of the land, in order to make more moral laws, thus creating a more "Christian" society?

Now, right in the middle of the Beatitudes is a command to seek justice and to make peace. What does that mean? Is that a call to use political action to bring peace in the world? If so, it would be an odd command from the same Jesus who told His disciples about the impending apocalypse and that the world would get a whole lot worse before it got better. Not only that, but implicit in the message of this same Jesus is the idea that the world will not get more just or more peaceful until He returns with a sword to make it so! In the meantime, He told His disciples to embody the characteristics of His life and ministry during His first advent.

The Beatitudes can be understood in a few ways. Some have said they are something like a code of ethics for Christians. Some biblical scholars have interpreted them to be a contrast between the superficial religious lives of the Pharisees with the deeper faith that Christ demands of His followers. While both of these interpretations have validity, I am convinced that the Beatitudes are primarily a contrast between Kingdom values and worldly values. You can't cherry pick through the Beatitudes and say "Well I like the seeking justice and peace part and I'll do that through political involvement. But I don't like the mourning or humility part. That's too sissy-ish. I prefer a Jesus that can kick some butt." The Beatitudes must be taken as a whole. They describe what we should be like as Christ's followers.

They are a portrait of what a follower of Jesus should look like in his or her actions. They are a way of life. They are not cold instructions. They are the living breathing embodiment of what it looks like to imitate Jesus in this world. The modern culture warrior mentality, on the other hand, is too distinctly American to be representative of the universal gospel. God is calling His Church first to bear spiritual fruit. Just as the Apostle Paul writes in Romans so Jesus throughout the Gospels, makes it clear that the fundamental purpose of the Gospel is to transform sinners into eternally Kingdom-minded followers of Him.

The way of Jesus is about strapping on your sandals, picking up your walking stick, and imitating the Master of Mercy in bringing hope, healing, and eternal life into this temporal, broken, dying world. We seem to have forgotten that the way of Jesus is a narrow way of imitating Christ. Unlike the church in America today, Jesus never engaged in political debate, intrigue, or shaped a people by way of legal coercion. He transformed sinners one at a time into citizens of an eternal Kingdom.

Look at the second principle I've gleaned from Paul's words in Romans Chapter One. The way of Jesus is a way of faith. Faith moves mountains. Faith moves mountains of despair. It shakes cultures by transforming hearts, not laws or public policies. I'm not saying that revival in any land may not lead to a change in laws. It should. If more people in America were in love with God they would be far less likely to allow abortion on demand to continue, for example. But take that logic in reverse. Seek revival in the hearts of men by living out a radical kind of Kingdom lifestyle of humility, peace, kindness, and authentic love in Jesus' name and then revival can happen.

We are going about the problems in the culture all wrong. We haven't earned a hearing with individuals on the basis of love to confront their sin with truth. We are demanding a hearing with society through public political action. But the Apostle Paul says "This Good News tells us how God makes us right in His sight. This is accomplished from start to finish by faith" (Romans 1:17). If our motives to engage in culture wars are godly, and I believe that by and large they basically are, then to glorify God in society and encourage a more moral and Christian populace, the only way to win that battle is to start and finish with faith.

What if we spent as much time praying for a specific individual's salvation as we do watching Fox News? What if every time we felt a tirade about the good old days coming on we paused and prayed for this current lost generation that is so far from God? I'm not implying that Christians today need to disengage the culture. *Far from it.* I'm saying that we need to use the right weapons and fight the right battles.

> *Put on all of God's armor so that you will be able to stand firm against all strategies of the devil. For we are not fighting against flesh-and-blood enemies, but against evil rulers and authorities of the unseen world, against mighty powers in this dark world, and against evil spirits in the heavenly places.*
> (Ephesians 6:11-12)

We are at war with sin and Satan, not sinners held captive by Satan. We are liberators with the Gospel, not God's present judgment on sinners. They haven't sinned against us but God. We (believers) are in the same boat with them (unbelievers). The only difference is that deliverance has come to us by faith in Jesus. The Kingdom mandate, when it comes to the vileness of culture, is the same as it has ever been. Our mission in the world is to reflect the love and beauty of Jesus – first by participating in genuinely authentic Christian community and then to open the doors of our meeting houses to let the light of Christ's love pour out onto the streets.

> *Bless those who persecute you. Don't curse them; pray that God will bless them. Be happy with those who are happy, and weep with those who weep. Live in harmony with each other. Don't be too proud to enjoy the company of ordinary people. And don't think you know it all! Never pay back evil with more evil. Do things in such a way that everyone can see you are honorable. Do all that you can to live in peace with everyone.* (Romans 12:14-18)

This brings us to Paul's third point in Romans Chapter One and my final point in this section. The Kingdom of God is an upside down kingdom. We are to bless our enemies, not go on Piers Morgan and blast them! We are to live peaceably with everyone. Who are the "all" referred to in this passage? Are they fellow believers, the world, or both? As a former seminary professor of mine used to say, "All means all. That's all all means!" What place does the culture warrior mentality have for Kingdom citizens?

The Bible says that vengeance belongs to God. Yet, it isn't hard to find a professed follower of Jesus spewing vitriol anger at the sinful culture he finds himself entangled in. We are fellow scoundrels with the world. The only difference between us and them is that we have been pardoned by the immense grace of God. Our mission isn't to condemn the culture but to act as a savory element, preserving and bringing life into it. Our ultimate call is to reflect the compassion and mercy of Jesus while proclaiming truth.

The mandate of the Church and every Christian is not "Conquer the world in Christ's name." It is be conquered by Christ and reflect His beauty in this world. George Eldon Ladd, in his book, *The Gospel of the Kingdom* writes, "The taking up of the cross is something which takes place in the depths of the human spirit and is fundamental to one's relationship to Christ. If I am ready to die for Christ, then my life is not my own, it is His."[5] That is what is at stake in this discussion. Does my heart belong to Christ or myself? I am surrendering my affections to Christ or to Caesar and his diabolically dastardly, entangling world systems.

The only war in this world, fought in anything resembling this world's terms, is the final battle to be waged by Christ upon His return to the world. In the meantime, we are called to reflect the pure beauty of the love of Christ in this world. We are to reflect the portrait of Christ exemplified at the cross — loving our enemies and praying for those who persecute and use us.

We need more praise — less politics. God doesn't need our vote. He wants our heart. Culture war engagement on the part of the follower of Jesus is little more than acquiescence to the spirit of religious moralism. It always fails. When the Church makes her aim the moral censure of a morally bankrupt society, Christians suffer a devolved form of spiritual piety and society receives a false witness as to the true nature of the Gospel of Jesus Christ.

> *You may think you can condemn such people, but you are just as bad, and you have no excuse! When you say they are wicked and should be punished, you are condemning yourself, for you who judge others do these very same things. And we know that God, in His justice, will punish anyone who does such things. Since you judge others for doing these things, why do you think you can avoid God's judgment when you do the same things?* (Romans 2:1-3)

I'm not saying don't care about the country or take part in its processes. I'm saying guard your heart. Care infinitely more about the Kingdom.

---

5   Ladd and George Eldon, *The Gospel of the Kingdom*, reprinted 2003 (Grand Rapids, Michigan: Wm. B. Eerdmans Publishing Company, 1959), 105.

The culture war mentality seems to be a natural byproduct of an egocentric American worldview. It is common within the churches in America and in the minds and hearts of most Americans.

Christianity is assumed by a lot of folks in our land whose lives and beliefs are at war with any historical or biblical notion of orthodox Christian belief and lifestyle. Growing up in North Central California I had a lot of friends who called themselves Christians.

"What religion are you?" one boy might ask another.

"Oh, we're Christians."

"Really? Where do you go to church?"

"We don't."

Christianity is assumed as the national religion on the part of many folks in our culture. Many others are pushing against that notion and embracing what is commonly called the "New Atheism." It's really nothing new at all but it sounds catchy and sells as many Christian polemic books as it does atheist books. It all makes for good business. But more to my point, there still remains a high segment of the population that believes themselves to be Christians because they are from America, are basically good people, and Grandma took them to church as a child.

They show up in the churches once in a while when life is rough, when they need financial assistance or at Christmas to see Cousin Susie sing in the Christmas cantata. These folks are glaringly inconsistent in the churches but their spirit is found throughout the churches. They are basically civic Christians. They are in favor of prayer at football games. They halfheartedly believe the core doctrines of the Christian faith, or at least what they think are the core doctrines of the Christian faith. But even their cousins that are regularly in the church pews hold a great deal in common with them.

Civic religion is alive and well in the hearts of occasional churchgoers, who like the idea of God and country, and it is alive and well in many supposed orthodox churches. A lot of would-be followers of Jesus are more like keepers of the grounds. They are less involved with the movement of the way of Jesus and more concerned with keeping the cemetery clean and well-groomed at the facility they grew up in with a cross on the steeple. They keep the flag clean. They keep the communion plates polished. They get upset if the pastor fails to preach a patriotic sermon near the 4th of July and they'd run him out of town, tarred and feathered, if he suggested removing the flag from the sanctuary.

I'm convinced that the basis for civic Christianity in America is rooted in a false belief that America has a particularly unique biblical role. There is really nothing in history or the Bible to warrant such a belief. God has used the Christians in this nation over the years to accomplish many things for His glory. Although, for as much good as the American church has done in exporting the Gospel through foreign missions, we have also exported materialism and greed.

That discussion aside, here is the biggest problem with the assumed belief that we are something like the new Israel or God's Israel for the modern era. When these kinds of false beliefs permeate our culture and the body of Christ, it necessarily follows that the church would see its primary mandate to transform society morally rather than to be transformed completely and wholeheartedly given over to the centrality of Christ in our hearts, minds, and subsequent actions. In this scenario, we become the Pharisees of America.

America is not God's instrument for spreading the Gospel in the world. That job is solely the work of the Holy Spirit working through the Church. There is only one biblical example of sanctioned conquest. Israel. And we see that the very notion of any nation of this world having a particular claim to divine authority in its warrior conquests ceased with the coming of Christ. The only mention of any future war being holy and divine is that of the return of Jesus mentioned in the book of Revelation.

The American way is centered more on greed and materialism than it is on any overtly biblical principle. Again, America may very well be the advocate for many societal or government positions that are much more moral than alternatives in the world but that does not make them on a par with or even remotely comparable to the ideals found in the Gospels. Guard your hearts.

For some Christians, it's as though George Washington is our Moses and the United States Constitution is the Ten Commandments. We march on the American flag at the start of worship services around the 4th of July and Veterans Day. On these same holidays, our pastors preach sermons comparing the sacrifice of Jesus with that of American soldiers. I'm making these observations from the inside, as an evangelical pastor. The most troubling thing is that I believe it to be on the level of our assumptions and so pervasive as to barely be noticed. I have for years felt the pressure from politically motivated Christian organizations sending me material and calling me and other evangelical pastors, urging us to take a stand on moral issues from the pulpit.

We even see whole large groups of evangelical pastors intentionally mocking tax law with annual Sundays given over completely for the purpose of political dialogue. I decided to become engaged in this discussion after I began to seriously question why the church in America seems so concerned with politics in America. What I'm saying in this section would have sounded like an unreasoned rant if someone else had written it even a few years ago. I didn't "get" the thoughts driving this discussion until it hit home on a Sunday evening just prior to the 2012 presidential election.

That evening I was approached by a Christian man who I love and respect, though I was surprised by the brashness of the request he laid on me. He came to me very concerned as to why I had not endorsed Mitt Romney's presidential candidacy from the pulpit. I explained to him that as a matter of conscience I don't get involved in politics in the capacity of the pastor of a local church. As such, I reserve pulpit time for distinctively sacred matters of Christian discipleship in terms of bearing fruit to the eternal Kingdom of God. I am a pilgrim in this world and have no desire to get too entangled with its affairs.

He was noticeably jumbled. His response highlighted to me the fact that many genuine believers in Jesus Christ today have had their allegiances so co-opted by nationalistic upbringings and political ideologies that they cannot separate the categories of their allegiance to the Kingdom of God and the kingdoms of this world. The notions of "God and Country" are fused in their minds in a way that makes them nearly inseparable.

He kindly accepted my answer with a shake of the head. He didn't get it. He is a kind and loving man so he let it go. His attitude is a great deal more Christ-like than some other folks I've encountered in the churches who are of a similar God and Country mindset. He assumes that because I am conservative biblically that I must line up with his political assumptions and, in point of fact, those of the Republican Party. He has bought the political banter of "Take America Back for God" hook, line, and sinker. He loves Jesus but doesn't have the same view of the world that God does. His internal allegiance seems plainly to be as much for America as it is for God.

There's nothing wrong with wanting to see one's homeland prosper. There is nothing wrong with honoring veterans. But there is something very wrong with placing the prosperity of any kingdom of this world on a par with or even above the Christian's call to bring Glory to God, our primary task in the world. There is something terribly wrong when concern for keeping our affections purely reserved for God, who is Lord of every kingdom and whose Kingdom is not of this world, is secondary to concern over the affairs of this world's systems. Guard your heart.

The very notion of a Christian nation is messed up like a football-bat.

Nations can't turn the other cheek. Nations can't love their enemies in this fallen world; at least not with despots in power and even good men trying to wade through messy geo-politics. The American government has even made some unique contributions to ideals held dear to most Christians. It has extended a high degree of freedom in the world. But it has also made many mistakes and all governments act in their own best interest. Just because America as a national entity is more benevolent than many, doesn't make it holy.

For as Kingdom citizens, we've got to get out of the good guy/ bad guy syndrome. We need only to understand the lost sinner/ saved sinner paradigm. America is not uniquely on God's side. Many in the Church and outside the Church today assume that we are because of the way history has been taught. The notions of manifest destiny and One Nation Under God have misled us to the assumption that whatever America does is inherently good and just, or at least her motives are always good and just. Even when the consequences of her actions are less than just we give ourselves a free pass because we believe ourselves to be the good guys.

The trouble with this way of thinking is that it keeps American Christians from having a distinctly Christian worldview. If we are in fact the new Israel, then what need is there for holiness in the Church? We don't need more holiness. We need more patriotism and more political leaders who think like us to bring the culture back in line with our notion of American-centered Christianity, which is, in fact, little more than a new brand of civic religion, that looks very little like the Kingdom of Heaven centered movement that Jesus preached.

When the hearts of Christians are too closely aligned to the historical narrative of this, or any nation their hearts are too easily kept from the only thing that should truly capture their hearts and imaginations – Christ and His Kingdom. I'm not going to go much further into this discussion in this treatment. The point is this: The church needs to go a lot deeper than civic religion. We need a revival of Holy Spirit-empowered, Christ-centered God-glorifying separation from the world's systems, and engagement with the world one sinner at a time in love with the truth of the Gospel.

I love America. And the very best thing for her is a healthy Holy Spirit-empowered church that is so utterly concerned with saving the lost and bringing glory to God through righteous living, that it barely has time to take notice who holds the current elected office or what recent political rabble filled the airwaves. If revival broke out in our land, within a few years those offices would be filled with people influenced or a part of a radical movement of followers of Jesus, as opposed to Americans under the delusion that growing up in a land with a church edifice on every street corner and hearing someone pray a prayer at the opening of the baseball game makes one a Christian.

Again, to be clear, I am of course not advocating here a dismissal of religious faith in the public forum. For the last few years I have written a weekly religious column in an overtly Christian fashion in a local newspaper. We should engage the public in every way possible. But we should engage the heart of God first and guard our allegiances. Whether we pray in school or not, whether we have authentic Christians in office or not, we must concern ourselves with fervent prayer in the Christian homes and offer an example of Christ in the world in our humble, genuine, bold, witness to the God who saves sinners through faith in Jesus Christ.

We need revival a great deal more than we need Christians in public office. We need Christ in the heart of the His Church more than we need Christians in any place. We need the kind of revival that Leonard Ravenhill prayed and preached for so many years in America before departing this life for Heaven. "Revival is the willingness to forsake all – that God might be all-in-all to the individual and to the Church."[6]

DON'T BUY A FALSE HOPE

There is an epidemic of anxiety in the churches today. And at least a significant part of this is the fact there is no peace for the Christian stuck on the Rush Limbaugh or Alan Combs political debate merry go round. The new life means righteousness and peace and joy in the Holy Spirit (Romans 14:17). There is encouragement

6   Ravenhill, Leonard, *America is too Young to Die* (Minneapolis, Minnesota: Bethany Fellowship Inc, 1979), 70.

in Christ (Philippians 2:1) and in humble service (Philippians 2:5). The peace of God guards the hearts and minds of those who are in Christ (Philippians 4:7). Paul can be content in every kind of human situation in Christ (Philippians 4:13).[7]

Hope is found in Christ alone and exemplified in pure Christian community. Christian community is distinct from general society or even our general connectedness as human beings. The fusion of Christianity and political ideology today rests, at least partially, on the assumption that making a better society somehow brings glory to God or, more specifically, brings God's goodness to bear in the world. Surely a more Christian society is better for the world but the world will never and can never be truly Christian.

God's creation of all humanity makes us one with the world only in a very broad and general sense. We share human pain and joy in common with all people. But only in Christian community do we share Christ. And Christian community can only exist among those who have been transformed by Christ. Outside of having received the sin-breaking, life-changing power of the Cross, people cannot be free to share in the hope that comes from Christians sacrificing and suffering for one another. The kind of Kingdom society that Jesus brings cannot exist apart from the life-giving, moving-power of the Holy Spirit.

Every Christian who makes it their burden to cling to political leaders and to press political ideologies, as though they have the power to bring more hope into the world, will only find him or herself filled with more anxiety and less peace. The hope of Christ can only be found in distinctly Christian gatherings of transformed sinners. That hope can never be pressed into or pushed upon the kingdoms of the world, no matter how hard or sincerely we press.

We decry society for taking Christ out of Christmas but we have removed Him from Christian discipleship. We condemn the

---

7   Ladd and George Eldon, *New Testament Theology* (Grand Rapids, Michigan: William B. Eerdmans Publishing Company, 1974), 481.

immorality common in the world instead of living holy lives as a people apart from the world. We are filled with anxiety because we are filled with every kind of care of this world. Caesar has taken something that is not his – our affections – and consequently, we are filled with anxiety.

Speaking of the need for the Christian to find his source of pure comfort and peace from God alone, John Wesley said it this way:

> My soul, thou canst not be fully comforted, nor have perfect delight but in God, the comforter of the poor, and the helper of the humble. Wait a while, O my soul, wait the Divine promise, and thou shalt have abundance of all good things. Use temporal things, desire eternal.[8]

"Use temporal things, desire eternal." Those words are striking to me. We are in the world and of the world. Our prayers are more centered on God glorifying America than they are God glorifying Himself through every tribe and tongue and people. My hope and prayer is that what I've written may serve simply as a central study on the core of what Jesus taught on the subject of being His disciple and being a citizen of an earthly kingdom. Jesus calls His followers to a distinctly different agenda than that of the world. We will not be free in our following of Jesus to any greater degree than to the degree to which we are in, but not of, this world.

When we fight against the world we lose the current battle for souls that is to be fought with Satan and we lose the war for internal freedom that was already won at Calvary. Christ died to set sinners free. We should walk in peace and freedom as followers of Christ.

---

8   John Wesley, *The Christian's Pattern* (Salem, Ohio: Schmul Publishers, 1975), 67.

It's a fine line to walk being in the world and not of the world. But that's where we have to live and breathe and share life with one another and do life in front of the world.

> "When we're unbalanced, we're not only irrelevant but we're a threat to ourselves and those around us. The world is filled with people who have been wounded by out-of-balance Separatists and Conformists. I have been, and I'll bet at times you have too. Sadly, I've been the one doing the wounding at times. We need to stop pretending that this doesn't happen. It does – often – and it discredits both Christ and his church."[9]

When we are overly engaged in political debates and striving for this candidate or the next, we give false witness to the world about the purpose and meaning of the Gospel. How does one define "overly" engaged? I'm not certain there is an easy answer to that question. On the one hand you have theonomists. These are a small but significant segment of the church in American that believe there is basically no such thing as being overly involved. They affirm political involvement as a means of fulfillment of their eschatological (second coming of Jesus) perspective and see political engagement as a means of ushering the literal Kingdom of God by transforming and taking over society.

On the other hand, you've got people like the Brethren Churches and others of the Anabaptist family of churches in America (Dunkers, Quakers, Mennonites) who go so far as to nearly or entirely remove themselves from modern society. I'm not advocating either of these extremes. Though were I to err I would do so in the direction of the separation from the world entirely. The balanced follower of Jesus lives somewhere in the tension – between the two positions.

---

9   Oberbrunner and Kary, *The Fine Line* (Grand Rapids: Zondervan, 2008), 65.

He is neither out of this world nor married to it. He is in the world but not of the world. He loves God and wants to make an impact in the world but loves God far too much to have his affections robbed away in political or social debates which have no end in sight. He embodies the admonition of Romans 12:9. "Don't just pretend to love others. Really love them. Hate what is wrong. Hold tightly to what is good." He is a rare find because if the responses of the world around us are any indication, most of us are not very balanced at all on this matter.

> Christianity has an image problem. We can deny it, disdain it, and decry it, but the fact remains: in our culture the church is perceived as caring more about insiders than outsiders. We've brought this upon ourselves largely as a result of evangelicalism's successful campaign to become America's leading purveyor of religious goods and services.[10]

I remember one evening at a church meeting. I informed the congregation, well the fifteen percent or so who had bothered to come to this all church business meeting, that I believed we needed to be more welcoming to visitors. A man in the church meeting interjected "We're a friendly church!" I informed him that while I appreciated his belief that we were a friendly church I had evidence to the contrary. I had spoken to a couple who'd been coming to church for several months and had only been welcomed by a handful of people assigned to that task.

His reply, "We're a friendly church!" I went on to explain several instances where this couple had been talked about but not talked **to** by people seated only a few feet away. I gave him and the rest of those gathered more than a few specific concrete examples. His reply this time? "We're a friendly church!" This was followed by a look to me that silently said "And shut up!" in the most friendly

---

10   Jim Henderson, Todd Hunter, and Craig Spinks, *Outsider Interviews* (Grand Rapids, Michigan: Baker Books, 2010), 31.

possible manner. Often, as I explained at this point, there is a difference between how we perceive ourselves and others perceive us.

Too often we come off like we have all of the answers. Christians are not wiser than nonbelievers. We are clusters of sinners, collected by God, and saved by His grace. What if, instead of passing ourselves off as the world's answer to all of its problems, we stuck to answering eternal questions? Is it true that because of our Christian faith we know what is best for the world in every area and sphere of life? We aren't of this world. We should be focused on eternal things and bringing the eternal perspective of God to bear in the spheres where He commands us to act. "Pure and genuine religion in the sight of God the Father means caring for orphans and widows in their distress and refusing to let the world corrupt you" (James 1:27).

I'm not saying you can't care about the affairs of the kingdoms of this world. I'm saying that many of us have replaced care for this world for care for our calling in Christ. We have traded a distinctly Kingdom of God identity for a civic religion of vaguely Christian morality fused with a kind of Clark Kent view of doing the right thing. We are good people and that is greatest downfall. Rather than being really bad people falling on the grace of God for everything and living a Kingdom commanded lifestyle, we are fairly good people who are too busy saluting flags at baseball games to put our arms around the poor, the cast out, and the lost that Jesus commands us to love.

We act as though we are better than others. When it comes to politics we insist that our candidate is God's candidate. This implies that we are better than other people. Our candidates have been found out as frauds at no lesser a rate than other candidates. How many of our candidates are actually only shrewd politicians who tout their Christian faith in order to garner that segment of the vote?

We act as though the Christian community is a perfect model. Christian community embodies pure ideals but we don't live them out very well. We point to a coming Kingdom that should be the center of our focus and message but when we sling slogans like "take America back for God" the world looks on and rightly asks "When was America ever entirely for God?" Was it when Christians owed slaves? Perhaps it was when white Christians employed children in their factories during the industrial revolution or disallowed blacks from eating at the same lunch counters? Because it certainly isn't today when professed Christians are as likely as anybody to be consumed with consumerism.

But all of this is somewhat anecdotal. More importantly, God has given us a clear mission and it has nothing to do with politics.

Our way of interacting with the world is defined by the way of Jesus. That way is the path of living out the Great Commission with our hearts given over to the Great Commandments. Our calling to change the world is to do so with the truth in love. By the way: sharing the truth in love with the world doesn't mean using the truth like a hammer on people's sin then sprinkling in a little salt by saying "but I say it in love." The Gospel truth is not a hammer. It is the anvil upon which God shapes all repentant sinners with the hammer of His corrective merciful love.

Before we can speak the truth in love we have to earn a hearing by entering into relationships with individual sinners, like us. Then we lovingly speak the truth into their lives. "Instead, we will speak the truth in love, growing in every way more and more like Christ, who is the head of His body, the church" (Ephesians 4:15).

We are called to serve the world, not wield political influence. As we examined above, the Great Commission is our ultimate mandate. And that mandate isn't to take America back for God or to be watchmen on political walls. Changed hearts in the world will only come on the heels of the proclamation in word, deed, and spirit of the Gospel. What has the last three decades of active campaigning on the side of conservative politics gained the church in America? What has lobbying for social justice gotten the liberal churches in American? As a society we are less moral *and* less just.

Perhaps instead of taking America back for God, it's time to take God back from America. The church in America today needs to walk out the Sermon on the Mount more and march less on Capitol Hill.

We are called to engage sinners one repentant heart at a time, not change society through political influence. Look at the example of Jesus. He got engaged in the lives of sinners. He doesn't push them away because of their sin. He pulls them to Himself because of the very fact that they are sinners! They need the love, mercy, compassion, and forgiveness that only He can offer.

Guard your heart. Don't sell a false witness of the politically motivated church. "There is nothing to gain in winning elections if we lose our soul in the process."[11]

---

11   David Kinnaman and Gabe Lyons, *Unchristian* (Grand Rapids, Michigan: Baker Books, 2007), 166.

WORKS CITED

Banks, Adelle M. "Franklin Graham Apologizes For Doubting Obama's Faith." *Christian Century.* 129, no. 6 (2012, January 01). ATLA Religion Database with ATLASerials, EBSCOhost, viewed 9 December 2013.

Henderson, Jim, Todd Hunter, and Craig Spinks. *Outsider Interviews.* Grand Rapids, Michigan: Baker Books, 2010.

Kinnaman, David, and Gabe Lyons. *Unchristian.* Grand Rapids, Michigan: Baker Books, 2007.

Ladd, George Eldon. *The Gospel of the Kingdom.* Reprinted 2003. Grand Rapids, Michigan: Wm. B. Eerdmans Publishing Company, 1959.

———. *New Testament Theology.* Grand Rapids, MICHIGAN: William B. Eerdmans Publishing Company, 1974.

"Lewrockwell.com," Jeff Barr, accessed December 10, 2013 March 17, 2010, http://www.lewrockwell.com/2010/03/jeffrey-f-barr/render-unto-caesar-amostmisunderstood-newtestamentpassage.

Oberbrunner, and Kary. *The Fine Line.* Grand Rapids: Zondervan, 2008.

Ravenhill, Leonard. *America is too Young to Die.* Minneapolis, Minnesota: Bethany Fellowship Inc, 1979.

———. *Revival Praying.* Minneapolis, Minnesota: Bethany Fellowship, 1962.

Rosscup, James E.. *Abiding in Christ.* Grand Rapids: Zondervan, 1973.

Stott, John R.. *The Message of the Sermon on the Mount.* Downers Grove, Illinois: Inter-varsity Press, 1978.

Wesley, John. *The Christian's Pattern.* Salem, Ohio: Schmul Publishers, 1975.

TOPICAL LINE DRIVES

Straight to the Point in under 44 Pages

All Topical Line Drives volumes are priced at $4.99 print and 99¢ in all ebook formats.

Available

The Authorship of Hebrews: The Case for Paul	David Alan Black
What Protestants Need to Know about Roman Catholics	Robert LaRochelle
What Roman Catholics Need to Know about Protestants	Robert LaRochelle
Forgiveness: Finding Freedom from Your Past	Harvey Brown, Jr.
Process Theology: Embracing Adventure with God	Bruce Epperly
Holistic Spirituality: Life Transforming Wisdom from the Letter of James	
	Bruce Epperly
To Date or Not to Date: What the Bible Says about Pre-Marital Relationships	
	D. Kevin Brown
The Eucharist: Encounters with Jesus at the Table	Robert D. Cornwall
Render to Caesar	Chris Surber
The Caregiver's Beattitudes	Robert Martin
What Is Wrong with Social Justice	Elgin Hushbeck, Jr.
The Authority of Scripture in a Postmodern Age: Some Help from Karl Barth	
	Robert D. Cornwall

Forthcoming

God the Creator: The Variety of Christian Views on Origins	Henry Neufeld
I'm Right and You're Wrong	Steve Kindle
Why Christians Should Care about Their Jewish Roots	Nancy Petrey

Planned

A Cup of Cold Water	Chris Surber
Christian Existentialism	David Moffett-Moore
Paths to Prayer	David Moffett-Moore

(The titles of planned volumes may change before release.)

Generous Quantity Discounts Available
Dealer Inquiries Welcome
Energion Publications — P.O. Box 841
Gonzalez, FL 32560
Website: http://energionpubs.com
Phone: (850) 525-3916

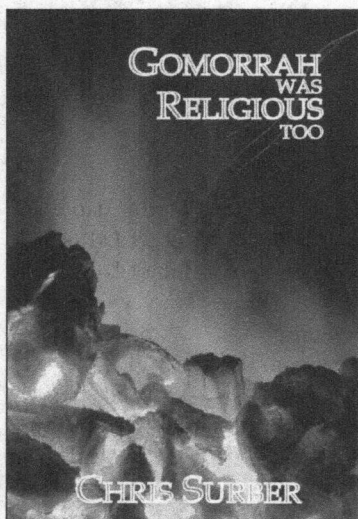

GOMORRAH WAS RELIGIOUS TOO

CHRIS SURBER

This book may be the catalyst for revival that the Church so desperately needs. I pray that all who read it would catch the spark that drives the author; and that Christ would fan those sparks into a great flame of revival in His Church.

Lawrence E. Bray Th.D
President, The North American Reformed Seminary

BY ROBERT D. CORNWALL

Your book is a great combination of a thoughtful sermon and an enjoyable personal conversation.

Gregory Wismar
Pastor
Christ the King Lutheran Church
Newtown, CT

THE SACRED JOURNEY
CHRIS SURBER

More from Energion Publications

Personal Study

Finding My Way in Christianity	Herold Weiss	$16.99
The Jesus Paradigm	David Alan Black	$17.99
When People Speak for God	Henry Neufeld	$17.99

Christian Living

Faith in the Public Square	Robert D. Cornwall	$16.99
Grief: Finding the Candle of Light	Jody Neufeld	$8.99
Crossing the Street	Robert LaRochelle	$16.99

Bible Study

Learning and Living Scripture	Lentz/Neufeld	$12.99
From Inspiration to Understanding	Edward W. H. Vick	$24.99
Luke: A Participatory Study Guide	Geoffrey Lentz	$8.99
Philippians: A Participatory Study Guide	Bruce Epperly	$9.99
Ephesians: A Participatory Study Guide	Robert D. Cornwall	$9.99
Evidence for the Bible	Elgin Hushbeck, Jr.	

Theology

Creation in Scripture	Herold Weiss	$12.99
Creation: the Christian Doctrine	Edward W. H. Vick	$12.99
Ultimate Allegiance	Robert D. Cornwall	$9.99
History and Christian Faith	Edward W. H. Vick	$9.99
The Church Under the Cross	William Powell Tuck	$11.99
The Journey to the Undiscovered Country	William Powell Tuck	$9.99
Eschatology: A Participatory Study Guide	Edward W. H. Vick	$9.99
Philosophy for Believers	Edward W. H. Vick	$14.99
Christianity and Secularism	Elgin Hushbeck, Jr.	$16.99

Ministry

Clergy Table Talk	Kent Ira Groff	$9.99
So Much Older Then ...	Robert LaRochelle	$9.99

Generous Quantity Discounts Available
Dealer Inquiries Welcome
Energion Publications — P.O. Box 841
Gonzalez, FL 32560
Website: http://energionpubs.com
Phone: (850) 525-3916